'Brilliant, funny, witty, moving, a[...] Sight is a fantastic and incredibl[...] answers to some of life's deepest q[...] think. Interwoven with Andy's ow[...] a helpful roadmap for the spiritually curious — whether you [...] no idea what you believe, are interested in finding out more what Jesus is all about, or have a heart full of doubts and a head full of questions. You'll laugh, you'll have "Aha!" moments, you'll have loads to think about — and you'll find it a book you can't put down.'

Dr. Andy Bannister,
Head of Solas, Centre for Public Christianity

'Andy has the knack of talking about faith in a thoroughly enjoyable way. If you are considering the Christian faith or want to explain its merits to others, *Hidden in Plain Sight* is an approachable, humourous and thought-provoking read. Read it, enjoy it, respond to it and share it; you won't be disappointed.'

Cathy Madavan, Speaker and Communicator

'Andy Kind is a masterful communicator and *Hidden in Plain Sight* is a joy to read. Through a wonderful blend of honesty, comedy and cultural insight, this book takes you on a journey of discovery, which will have you snorting with laughter one moment and thinking deeply the next.'

Liam Thatcher, The Bible Society

'Andy Kind writes in a genre that does not exist. Or at least — it didn't until now. Somehow, he manages to be hilariously funny about life and deadly serious about God — all at the same time. How does he do it? I have no idea. But do it he does.'

Dr. Steve Burnhope, Theologian

HIDDEN IN PLAIN SIGHT

CLUES YOU MAY HAVE MISSED IN THE SEARCH FOR MEANING

Jacsy,

God Bless,

Andy Kind

ANDY KIND

ABOUT THE PUBLISHER

McKnight & Bishop are always on the lookout for new authors and ideas for new books. If you write or if you have an idea for a book, please email: **info@mcknightbishop.com**

Some things we love are undiscovered authors, open-source software, Creative Commons, crowd-funding, Amazon/Kindle, faith, social networking, laughter and new ideas.

Visit us at **www.mcknightbishop.com**

Cover image generously provided by
Peter Cutler (Zen Monk, Artist & Teacher)
www.zenartofenlightenment.com

Copyright © Andy Kind 2022
The rights of Andy Kind to be identified as the Author of this Work has been asserted by him in accordance with Section 77 of the Copyright, Designs and Patents Act 1988.

ISBN 978-1-905691-75.3
A CIP catalogue record for this book is available from the British Library.

First published in 2022 by McKnight & Bishop
35 Limetree Avenue, Kiveton Park, South Yorkshire, S26 5NY
http://www.mcknightbishop.com | info@mcknightbishop.com

This book has been typeset in Palatino Linotype and BEBAS NEUE
Printed and bound in Great Britain by Mixam, 6 Hercules Way, Watford WD25 7GS

This is for the one who really cared;
who was hidden in plain sight the whole time;
who I took too long to see,
and so missed.

And so miss.

Soooooooooooooo…

FOREWORD

BY GLEN SCRIVENER

Opening for a comedian is a thankless task. No-one's here for the MC. You've paid good money for the big name at the top of the bill, not some segue-peddling enthusiast asking if you're having a good night every 12 seconds. But Andy's asked me to say a few words while he gets ready backstage.

While we wait, I want to give my heartiest commendation of *Hidden In Plain Sight* (HIPS). This book is, in fact, a rare and dazzling gem. There really is nothing like it out there, and I can't think of a better use of the next hour of your life. I chuckled, hooted and guffawed my way through its pages. It's seriously funny and seriously thoughtful. A sensational combination.

As we prepare ourselves, let me reassure you: no prior knowledge of faith or philosophy is required. Andy won't so much be pointing you up to divine realities above. He won't so much be pointing you back to religious events in the past. Mainly he'll be doing what comedians do best: observing. He'll be pointing out the stuff that's all around. It's right under your nose: hidden in plain sight. And you will laugh because you'll see it again from another angle. The plain will become strange again and the ordinary will become wonderful, literally 'full of wonder.'

Wonder is in short supply right now, at least in the over 7s. Children find it everywhere. Introduce them to fireflies, water slides, waffles, dinosaur books, *Lego* spaceships, stories about naughty children and ridiculous adults, purring kittens or slobbering dogs and you'll see their eyes: big as manhole covers. Everything is awesome. At some point, though, it wears off. And one of the great spell-breakers is the big old stories we tell one another about 'the real world'. Apparently, in 'the real world' our wonder reduces to neuronal firings. Our psychology boils down to biology, which boils down to chemistry, which boils down to physics. 'The real world' is essentially a gazillion tiny billiard balls clacking together, and so are we. Tragic story, man. A real buzz kill.

But Andy's here to reawaken our wonder. It helps that he's a comedian. It also helps that he's a child - in the best possible sense. He wants us to notice the wonder and the awe that's hidden in plain sight. And he wants us to think: how is that wonder best accounted for? Are we merely biological survival machines, clinging to an insignificant rock, hurtling through a meaningless universe towards eternal extinction? Is that the Big Story to make sense of our Little Stories? Is that the lens through which we can best view life? Andy will give you a different frame of reference and say, 'Try this on for size.'

HIPS does not ask you to leave the rational, everyday realm and 'leap' towards some otherworldly 'faith'. You never need to leave the climate-controlled comforts of your own life experience. The invitation is simply to stay where you are and look around, to really take it in. Faith is simply seeing again - seeing the life you know in a different frame. The world you see remains the same. It's the same for you, for me, for everyone. But at some point you find a frame that brings it all into focus. Something clicks. And, like with the best joke, you *get it*. Faith and laughter are very similar. That's why this tour of life and faith is so necessary, and why Andy Kind is the perfect guide.

Anyway, I've gone on too long. Are you ready for our headline act? Now, Ladies and Gentleman, you're in for an absolute treat. Please give it up for **MR. ANDY KIND**...

TO BEGIN WITH...

'I UNDERSTOOD LONELINESS BEFORE I KNEW WHAT IT WAS.'
Giant by Rag'n'Bone Man

'WE DANCE AROUND IN A RING AND SUPPOSE,
BUT THE SECRET SITS IN THE MIDDLE AND KNOWS.'
Robert Frost

Greetings, friend!

Bit of a creepy way to start but it's too late to make any changes now. Come in out of the cold and take a seat by this fire, there's a tray of hot beverages around somewhere. Don't sit on the cat.

This blessedly short book is based on my national comedy tour of the same name, with some extra thoughts that didn't feature in the show because I just forgot, OK? It's a book which aims to offer a gentle and humble championing of the story of Christianity. Most people who write books attempting to argue for a particular worldview usually have various letters after their names. By contrast, I usually have Ketchup on my trousers, which isn't to overly downplay my ability to speak on the concept of God but simply to make you feel relaxed, if not completely superior, as we start. While I have been known to work hard on the odd occasion, I'm also the man who spent one Saturday in 2010 hiding in *Ikea* wardrobes and asking people for directions to Narnia. Impressive credentials, I'm sure you'll agree.

You don't need to know too much about me before we start, but I can decorate the scene with a few personal trinkets while we get comfortable. I like strong cheese and long walks and short stories and sending postcards where the final line is always 'P.S. Are you still planning to kill your postman?'

I am also a father, and am owned by two daughters named Alice and Heidi, whom I love more than even the strongest cheese or the shortest story. They are both homeschooled, which is going to make Prom night a bit of a wash-out but at least we'll save money on a dress. Becoming a Dad has really brought me into the presence of that curious power known as Unconditional Love - something I'll be focussing on in a short while. And it's true: my love for my daughters, my total commitment to them, is unswerving, not based on appearance or performance or whether they can successfully name the 2004 Arsenal 'Invincibles' team. Nothing can change my love for them, and realising that was the first step in wanting to write the show which became this book. Heidi was actually born without a little toe on her left foot, which hasn't affected her life in any major way; it just meant that, when she was a baby, singing 'This Little Piggy Went to Market' was something of an anti-climax.

Right, enough tittle tattle! Are you warm enough? Can I refill your glass? Then let's begin...

ORIGIN STORY

When I was 22[1], something happened to me that I didn't really expect or particularly want to happen: I became a Christian. It was maybe the second most surprising event I've ever witnessed. For context, the most surprised I have ever been was the moment I learned that saying 'Space Ghettos' in an American accent will make it sound like you're saying 'Spice Girls' in a Glaswegian accent. If you want to take a few moments to test that theory, be my guest.

It would be tempting to deceive you into thinking I was once a staunch atheist, the dramatic turnaround grandstanding the conversion narrative and psychologically manipulating you into accepting my story. But as you'll find as we go along, my story isn't the only thing that counts here: *yours is*. My experiences only have any relevance so far as they are also

---

1   *I'm currently 40 so this was a long time ago, back when both Woolworths and the Lost City of Atlantis were still easily accessible.*

your experiences. I begin with the belief that we share a lot of common ground, although I suspect your proudest achievement is something more impressive than beating your next door neighbour's teenage sons in a water fight despite overwhelming odds.[2]

So no, I was never an atheist; I always believed there was *someone* or *something* out there bigger than me. On my travels through life I've seen numerous signposts pointing to something beyond the physical and the material, and I have always found that intriguing. But signposts are not the destination. When I see the sign at Junction 15 of the M6 that says 'Welcome to Newcastle-under-Lyme', I don't pull over and hug the hoarding as though I was already at home with a plate of baked Camembert. But I know I'm going in the right direction.

Nevertheless, when I became a Christian (by which I really mean when I made a conscious choice to start following Jesus; when I went from liking to subscribing) part of me was devastated. At that point in my life - fresh out of university, single, relatively non-monstrous when it came to looks, most people still swiping left - I think I wanted something else to be true, another story that offered me less structure and more freedom. I liked those pictures where women in togas poured loads of wine over you and some of it went in your mouth and some of it splashed on the floor but that didn't matter because

---

2   *Outnumbered 3 to 1, they initially had the upper hand and the greater fire power. But once the kettle boiled I really came into my own.*

there were women in togas pouring wine on you. Honestly, if Bacchus the Roman God of Wine had seemed genuinely viable as a true story, I'd be writing a very different book.

The reason I think I wanted another story to be true is because owning the title of 'Christian' in 21st Century Western society is hard. It's not a particularly popular outfit to wear, culturally - kind of like turning up to a wedding wearing a tracksuit.

At various points along humanity's timeline, being a Christian was either expected, normative or non-contentious. Self-preservation, that strong desire to survive by huddling into a crowd, is a powerful driving force in how we as humans describe and label ourselves, and over a long period of time the tag of 'Christian' was the factory setting for a Western society. That doesn't mean that everybody calling themselves a Christian actually was one - in the same way that calling myself Christian Bale doesn't get me royalty cheques from Christopher Nolan's *Batman* trilogy - but simply that it was the default term for somebody who had a basic belief in God and wanted to live a good life. It was the password to social acceptance, if you like.

As the world has shrunk, as social media has given everyone a platform to voice their opinions and views - no matter how ill-informed they may be - and as biblical literacy (understanding what the Bible actually is and actually teaches) has diminished, the word 'Christian' is now a rather loaded term, straining under the weight of having endless assumptions dumped onto it, like Nachos ladled unfathomably with chilli beef when simple melted cheese is what they were designed for.

In the minds of many, Christianity is just an avatar for bigotry, intolerance, self-righteousness, hypocrisy, sandals with white socks - and plenty more. However unjustified I might find a lot of those tags, the sign theory of language (where the words we use create spontaneous mental pictures) guarantees that the moment I tell someone I'm a Christian their mind is flooded with a variety of images, assumptions, expectations and triggers, which may cause that person's internal flood defences to shoot up. When that happens, sharing my story and *my truth* can become impossible: whatever reasoning I try to put forward is likely to fail, no matter how valid; my wave of earnest and reasoned testimony breaks harmlessly against the sea wall. To put it another way, calling yourself a Christian is like being the unauthorised object in the bagging area.

If I had just wanted to 'fit in' as a young man, I wouldn't have allowed myself to become a Christian. Instead I would have called myself 'open-minded, curious, searching, spiritually-inclined, non-judgemental.' I don't know many people who actually *are* these things, but I know plenty who understand that self-labelling in such a way will offer them a degree of social safety. After all, nobody is going to pick an argument with someone who is 'open-minded and non-judgemental' without themselves coming across as closed-minded and judgemental. Finding your place in society is a live-action roleplay game.

A lot of my friends would call themselves atheists. I don't really think that they are; I think they just know that calling yourself an atheist is one of the current passwords to social acceptability and acceptance. It's expected, normative and non-contentious, and people just want to fit in. It's the Critical Hit in the current roleplay.

But you dig down far enough into almost anyone's thinking and you'll find their bedrock isn't Atheism. They might disbelieve in Christianity, or they may not have thought about it much at all, but they don't lack *belief* in a wider sense, and they have a conglomeration of core beliefs on which they are building their life.

Nevertheless, my friends (all of whom, for the purposes of this book, are named Mordecai) will say something like: 'Whilst I respect you as a person, Andy, and while I know you to be someone who would never do something so half-witted as overload a plate of Nachos with what is essentially Chilli con Carne, which, let's be brave enough to say it, is a totally separate meal to Nachos and destroys the entire dish by turning the tortillas into mush...while I respect all of that, I find Christianity to be totally ridiculous.' When this happens - when somebody tells me that the thing I believe above all things and cling to most fondly is ridiculous - I look them in the eye with steely confidence and say, 'Agreed, Mordecai, agreed!'

Because I do agree. I agree that Christianity is at least superficially ridiculous. I don't know to what degree you've stopped to think about it, but let me run this by you: the Creator of the universe is a person. This personal Creator came down in human form to *find* us, lived the perfect life, allowed himself to be executed and then, a few days later, rose from the dead, overturning death, thereby allowing us to have the relationship with that Creator that we were supposed to have and becoming the person we were born to be.

That's not just ridiculous - it's absolutely bonkers. It's *Arkham Asylum* insane. Please don't misunderstand me: I believe that particular story more than I believe any other, and my entire life is dedicated to sharing with people the idea that this is, in fact, the Big Story that the universe is telling. But it doesn't mean I don't think it's ridiculous. However, I'd like to unpack all this a bit more if you don't need to rush off?

It's at times like this that we need to upgrade our reasoning from the grainy, low-resolution thinking found on social media to something more high-definition. The early Greek philosophers (most notably Socrates and Plato) developed something called 'dialectic' - a discourse between people holding different views but wanting to establish the truth through reasoned discussion. This approach to disagreement worked well for hundreds of years. The Twitterisation of our culture, however, has replaced actual longform dialogue with a series of verbal spats. Truth is now a popularity contest, a survival of the retweetiest.

The temptation in our disastrously tribal, hair-trigger world might be to latch upon my use of the word 'ridiculous' and declare, 'Aha, you see, even the religious don't actually believe it! Olympus has fallen! The witch is dead!' But I'd like to invite us to try this crazy new fad called nuance.

You see, for something to be true I don't have to fully understand it. Something can seem ridiculous to me and still be true. I didn't come close to understanding the films *Tenet* or *Inception*, but I didn't leave the cinema thinking Christopher Nolan didn't exist. More recently, if someone had announced to me on New Year's Day 2020, 'By May this year, most of your shoes will assume you've been murdered,' that would have seemed unthinkable.

When I call something 'ridiculous' or 'stupid' or 'gorgeous', I'm saying at least as much about me as I am about the thing I'm referencing. If something can only be true once I personally understand it, what I'm essentially promoting is the idea that I am 'God'. I must be, because I am the ultimate root of knowledge and the final gauge of whether something is normal, acceptable, accessible etc. The good news for everyone is that I am not God. You would know if I were God because all socks would be remote-controlled and people who talked about their pets as though they were children would be put in prison and, depending on my mood, executed. The same applies to people who refer to their partners on Facebook as 'this one'. Eg. "Happy Birthday to this one, love you to the moon and back". Honestly, if you love them that much you could at least try to remember their name. Please stay on the moon.

The next thing to say is that, while I agree that Christianity is 'ridiculous' or bonkers or far-fetched, so is *literally* every other major worldview. By worldview, I simply mean the Big Story that each of us thinks best explains how the world works and why. That might be a religion, or a vague sense of spirituality, or Atheism. Sometimes it's a random mix of philosophies, parental hand-me-downs and *Star Wars* quotes, that we hang across our lives like garish bunting. But whichever worldview you want to look at, you are likely to reach a point where it stops making sense, where it becomes unfathomable and you're struggling to process it. Perhaps you hold the belief that all major worldviews are silly, because nobody sees or perceives *objective reality*. OK, but that in itself is a part of your worldview: it's the lens through which you see the world. Not everyone has a religion or even a life philosophy, but everyone has a worldview.

IN THE BEGINNING...

Let's take as an example the creation of the universe. Any worldview that wants to assert itself as true, any worldview that wants to stand up and declare 'I am Spartacus', needs at some point to engage and intersect with the origin story of the cosmos. Now, since the arrival of Big Bang cosmology in the 1960s we've known that the universe *began to exist* - it hasn't always been there. It's a bit smug to point out that the first line of the Bible has held that view for a few thousand years and science has now caught up, but it's not totally untrue. In that way the Bible is like the person (usually my Mum) who calls out the murderous fisherman in a Scandinavian Noir within the first 5 minutes and then sits there while everyone else in the room tries to disprove and throw scorn at such wayward sleuthing, only to concede in the final scenes that, 'OK, you were right, but you probably had some inside knowledge'. The fact that the opening line of the opening book of the Bible displays some insider knowledge might well be a modest clue in our search for truth and meaning.

So anyway, given that the universe began to exist at some point around 13.8 billion years ago, the science provides us with two - but only two - options. Option One is that the universe was created by *something or someone* outside of itself: something or someone that would have to be super-powerful, timeless, immaterial (not possessing a physical body); something or someone we might call god (notice the deliberate small 'g'). You may disdain and dislike Option One but fear not, my liege, for a solitary alternative avails you, which is this: the universe created itself out of nothing.[3]

Of course, we know from *The Sound of Music* that 'nothing comes from nothing; nothing ever could.' Julie Andrews taught us that and she's practically perfect in every way.

But those are our two options. Either the universe was created by a being approximate to a god, or out of nothing, *nothing* created *everything* for *no purpose*. Both of those views are 'ridiculous'. One of them is true.

Like it or not, one of those storylines holds the explanation for how everything you see and feel and touch and smell got here. And you get to decide which one of those ridiculous options you think makes more sense. As Glen Scrivener says,

---

3   *At this point I would have liked to include a gif of Jack Nicholson laughing like a maniac, but that technology hasn't been invented yet.*

'Christians believe in the virgin birth of Jesus; atheists believe in the virgin birth of the universe: pick a miracle.'

Bear in mind, we're not at Jesus Christ yet, so committing yourself to the 'god' option doesn't lumber you with things like talking snakes, Jewish zombies or old ladies filling cafetieres with instant coffee like absolute lunatics. But, all things being equal, which of those makes more sense to you? It's surely a problem for strict materialists (people who believe that the universe is purely physical matter) that nothing in creation could have created creation.

So, if we can at least acknowledge that all major worldviews are binky bonkers - if we can at least call it 0-0 - then we are still left with the rather strange reality that reality is real. *Something* about the universe is *true*. Life is a true story. It may not be a very good one (it may not be, in the words of Alan Partridge, *Bravo Two Zero* by Andy McNab) but your life is happening. The author G. K. Chesterton once wrote, 'I had always felt life first as a story: and if there is a story, there must be a story-teller.' The question for us, then, is: who is this storyteller? Who's writing this stuff? You might be the main character in your life, but who's the author?

Back to my own story. The reason I became a Christian was because I went searching for meaning and identity. I had lived a really happy, secure, untroubled life, eaten a load of cheese, been to a good school and then a good university, and had defied expectations by graduating despite absolute minimal work.[4] And then, having been cruising on autopilot at high altitude, I realised I was supposed to be piloting my own life and hadn't mastered the controls. Like a lot of people in their early twenties, I believed I could fly - R. Kelly told me that and he's practically p...he's a really bad example, actually.

I left university and realised that my questions about life were getting bigger, and some of the answers I'd taken for granted were shrinking, covering less ground. It wasn't that I wasn't inquisitive at uni, but I was pampered by academic structure and shielded by ready-made social groups. The biggest questions I was asking at Warwick University were: what flavour Pot Noodle shall I have for my breakfast? Who's my favourite member of S-Club 7?[5] Shall I wash my bedding this week or just *Febreeze* it again?

After university, in the cold light of adulthood and self-reliance, the storyline I'd been clinging to for a couple of decades began to seem like a fairy story, so I started looking around for inspiration. And I quickly learned something upsetting: our society is saturated with emotive slogans that sound oh-so-empowering, but which crumble over time like homemade biscuits. One of those phrases is 'You can be whatever/whoever you want to be.' That is not true - at all.

As a child, when people you trust to guide you through your early life like Albus Dumbledore insist that you can be

---

4   *My degree is another example of something coming from nothing.*

5   *Rachel.*

whatever or whoever you want to be, it sounds amazing - it's our 'You're a wizard, Harry!' moment. And for quite a long stretch of time it also appears feasible: you're growing and learning, developing gifts, forming alliances, overcoming monsters. You seem to be on that trajectory that you were promised. The prophecy shall come to pass.

But then you have to be an adult. You have to provide for yourself, to compete against other people just as entitled and empowered as you. Shouting *'Accio* happiness and a career!' doesn't work. You realise that you're not a wizard at all: you're a muggle, and your personal Dumbledores, who told you that you could be whatever you wanted, haven't travelled with you on your journey but are back where you started, telling the next influx of kids that anything is possible and magic is real.

I came out of university and I wanted to discover who I was. Even then, I think I had an idea that there *was* a person there to discover, not simply to invent. My identity was perhaps hidden, but it wasn't non-existent. I believed intuitively that finding your identity is archeology as much as architecture: you dig for it more than you build it - or you at least find where the foundations are! My friend Mordecai went off to Vietnam and Bali to 'find himself'. Implicit in that sort of common utterance is the idea that there really is a *you* to be found.

One of the quirks of humanity is that we all ask the same fundamental questions. Wherever and whenever we are from, the three questions that we have always asked as a species are to do with origin, purpose and destiny: Where did it all come from? Why am I here? Where am I going?

At that point in my early twenties I didn't really know what I thought of the Big Story that the universe is telling (and by 'Big Story' I simply mean whatever is ultimately true about the universe - the 'why' of existence). There seemed to be an infinite number of religions, philosophies and conspiracy theories which sought to account for how and why the universe is as it is, and I wasn't sure which of those Big Stories out there was the real deal. But I did know something about my 'Little Story', and it's to that that we now turn.

DOORS IN THE WALLS
OF THE WORLD

In my search for meaning, I knew that there were certain things that were true for me and about me, things that were binding and non-negotiable in my life, regardless of whatever else was stitched through the fabric of the cosmos. Here's a few examples...

I knew that I believed in Love. Not just love, but *Unconditional* Love. I wanted to be loved without fear of rejection; loved for who I was and not based on what I did.

I believed in Justice. I knew that some things were absolutely wrong, objectively and bindingly, whether anyone agreed with me or not. For instance, I knew that sexually abusing a child was ALWAYS wrong and NEVER a matter of opinion. And where such absolute wrongs existed, they should be put right, made just. The laws of nature can't create matter, they only describe how it works. In the same way, the moral law (our sense of right and wrong) doesn't create what matters - it merely frames it.

I believed in Purpose. I wanted my life to go somewhere and to be about something; to count for something.

I believed in Freedom. I wanted to be free, not enslaved.

I believed in Beauty. I knew that when I listened to beautiful music it was transcendental, taking me out of myself towards something else - something bigger. 'A sense sublime of something far more deeply interfused' as William Wordsworth wrote. Awe is simply the realisation that something is both real and bigger than you.

I believed that Death *felt* unnatural to observe, no matter how many times I observed it.

I knew that when I carried absolutely anything up a short flight of stairs I would always say, 'Well, I won't need to go to the gym today!' That's not the most important thing on this list, but truth is truth.

I knew about things like Hope and Joy. I didn't just understand how to use these words in conversation; I recognised and apprehended the sensations that fill you when these things are present. The Germans have a word, *sehnsucht*, which means a longing for something you can't quite grasp but yet you still desire it. Joy and Beauty create this longing in us.

What's really interesting is that all of these concepts are just as much part of *your* Little Story as they are mine. I'd be hugely surprised if you disagreed with anything on that list. You and I might hope *for* different things and find joy *in* different things, but Hope and Joy *feel* the same for you as they do for me. We don't invent these forms - we discover them, stumble across them, dig them up by mistake sometimes. But they are archeological, not architectural. And they are non-material, not measurable by apparatus, not repeatable by scientific experiment. They are doors in the walls of the physical world.

More than that, these qualities tend to be noticeable by their absence as much as by their presence. You know you believe in Unconditional Love when you feel rejected. You know you believe in Purpose when it seems as though your life is going nowhere. You know you believe in Freedom when you feel trapped - being trapped is simply the absence of Freedom.

These basic experiences pointed me to something beyond myself. They were symbols of identity. Now this is interesting: the word 'symbol' comes from a Greek term *symbolon*. In the ancient world, a symbolon was a clay seal which was broken in half and split between two people as a sign of identity. When the two halves were brought together, the true identity was recognised. So Love and Hope and Beauty and Freedom are symbols of identity, but I desired to know where the other half was, to satisfy my *sehnsucht*.

Words, just as much as universes, have origin stories. The word 'desire' itself comes from '*de sidere*' meaning 'from the stars', while the word ecstasy derives from '*ek stasis*' meaning 'outside yourself'. Even as I started wanting to know where these concepts pointed, the desire itself was a signpost in the right direction - a sort of spiritual sonar. There's that well-known trope from science fiction, found most notably in the film *Close Encounters of the Third Kind*, where our human satellites suddenly pick up on a signal from outer space; a signal which is distant, invisible, but somehow recognisable, somehow aimed *at us*.

Or, as Gandalf says to Frodo in *Lord of the Rings*, 'The ring wants to be found.'

And so what I wanted to know was this: was there a Big Story somewhere that made sense of my Little Story? And if so, which? What did these doors in the walls of the world open onto? When faced with the vastness of the universe and all its tangled ideas and phenomena, our response might well be one of curious baffledness. But none of us believe *nothing*. We all believe lots of things. Rene Descartes, regarded by many as the father of modern philosophy, believed that some things really could be known for certain. He scaled it down to the first principle of 'I think, therefore I am.' But I think we can go further. I love and hope and desire, therefore....*something*.

32

Off I went on my stuttering quest, setting off in search of real meaning and not just well-worn mottos or verbal placebos or family tradition. I went hunting for treasure...and stopped at a small hill in first century Palestine where X marked the spot.

I came to the conclusion that, actually, there's only one Big Story out there that comes anywhere near to making sense of my Little Story, and as frustrating as that was for the guy with Bacchus posters on his wall, it's the story of Christianity.

BLACK COFFEE, MILKY TRUTH

We need a shout of 'Cut!' here for some Director's commentary, I suspect. Christopher Nolan would be proud, if only he existed.

When I say 'the story of Christianity', I don't mean the claim from some quarters that people are evil for being gay, or that dinosaurs were invented by an advertising agency to sell toys, or even the idea that if you live a good life, eat your greens and don't swear, God will like you. There are so many false assumptions and warped ideas about what Christianity is (largely down to the fact that too many genuine believers think that God is there to vindicate their personal prejudices) and we don't have time to talk about that here, but it's enough to say that what I'm discussing is what JRR Tolkein called the 'true myth' of Christianity: the story where God came to find us in our brokenness and offered to carry us, fix us, love us. Against the backdrop of the bad news that the universe is bleak and mindless and ultimately meaningless, Jesus steps centre-stage and, arms stretched wide, stage-whispers the good news which is this: the bad news is a lie, and there's a better story.

So I became a Christian. And for the last 20 years or so I've been trying to share my belief that Christianity is the Big Story which the universe is telling with as many people as possible. And obviously that has proven to be a challenge - a challenge no less gargantuan than trying to confine yourself to a single Jaffa Cake. If you remember my earlier analogy, not only had I turned up to the wedding in a tracksuit but I was now trying to convince the other guests that they should consider dressing that way, too! As I look back on some of my early attempts to share my story, I would certainly want to write 'Could do better' in red ink somewhere in the margins. And I certainly wouldn't be inviting myself to any weddings.

I can't take all the blame though, you realise. It's not all my fault. A big problem in discussions about Big Stories is often that we can over-personalise the battle. If you and I went out for coffee (this one's on me, by the way) and we were discussing such matters - your initial interest morphing to disgust as I somehow find both the money and the stomach space for a fifth Millionaire's shortbread - at some point you might say:

'OK then, show me why you're right and I'm wrong.' Instantly, we're into a conflict situation where there will be a winner and a loser. And people tend to become very defensive in conflict situations. The Duke of Wellington said after the Battle of Waterloo that, next to a battle lost, the saddest thing was a battle won. He was wrong, of course - the saddest thing is always an empty cafetiere. But when discussions become conflicts, there's often more pain than healing, more heat than light.

So hopefully it's helpful and reassuring for me to say that I don't think *I'm right* and *you're wrong*. I am, no doubt, right and wrong about lots of things. For instance, it is my long-held and genuine belief that Arsenal Football Club is by far the greatest team the world has ever seen. Unfortunately for me, that is a demonstrably false belief, and yet I still cling to it. Contrariwise, I am definitely right that soup is disgusting and not real food - it's vegetable blood and a complete waste of a main course. And don't tell me that not all soup is vegetables, Mordecai - I have never once felt the desire to drink a chicken.

The truth or falsity of Christianity doesn't depend on what either you or I think about it. Whatever is true *out there* is independent of what my feelings on the issue may be. 'Facts don't care about feelings' is too combative a phrase, but there's something in it. The question is: what is the fact? What is that Big Story written into the cosmos?

So I don't think you're wrong. In fact, I think that you're right! In the sense that I agree on the existence of all these things we've been discussing: Love, Hope, Joy, Beauty, Purpose, Freedom etc. We both think these concepts are real and not made-up, not simply word games. When material comfort is stripped and ripped away - which, sorry to ladle truth soup into your bowl, it ultimately will be - it is these qualities which impregnate life with real meaning. My humble suggestion is not that your Little Story is faulty, but that perhaps your view of the Big Story needs changing. Because your Big Story might not agree with you about how the universe is ordered, or allow for some of the things your Little Story sees as obvious. And if that is the case - if you find that your Big Story doesn't agree with your Little Story - here's a cutesy idea: find a better one. We love and hope and cry, but we need to do it in the right direction.

Probably, at this point in our coffee shop patter, you would graciously calm the heck down and alter your question to: why is what you believe true? And honestly, that's a real zinger of a question. But this is where I think my younger and wildly-caffeinated Christian self over-complicated matters in his attempts to persuade people. For instance, I might have said something like, 'Let me tell you about some miracles!!!'[6]

---

6   *Let the extra exclamation marks assure you that my body has, by this point, yielded to the god of sugar. Again, note the small g.*

I do believe in miracles, and with good reason - I once pressed 'print' on a *Word* document and it actually printed. I wish you'd been there.

But yes, I believe in miracles. Specifically, I believe that, sometimes, God heals today. I regularly pray for people to be healed from various problems they're experiencing, and on several occasions folk have witnessed what they would call 'miraculous healing'. The problem when you start talking about healing, though, is that the whole issue yields more questions than answers, and I don't have time here to talk about that (this section is a cute little side mission but doesn't count towards 100% completion of the main story). The topic of healing is intriguing but it's also confusing, which is why I don't 'go large' on it when trying to persuade people of the truth of Christianity. However, let me give you just a couple of examples of people experiencing healing.

I was at an event on a campsite in Derbyshire, which is how all the classic novels have started. This was pre-pandemic when masks were for heists and creepy pagan dances. A lady walking across the campsite twisted her knee and fell to the ground in agony. VAR wasn't available so we have no idea whether it was deliberate or not, but she sat there in a lot of pain, unable to get up or to even bend the leg. She would tell me that this had happened to her twice before and that, on both occasions, she had needed to go to hospital with gas and air.

I decided I would pray for the knee. This may seem bizarre to you, but sometimes the things which cause us to back away or snear are simply those things for which we have no framework or concept...and so our feeling of insecurity creates a strong fight or flight response. The things that each of us call weird are simply those things that we don't experience in our day-to-day lives. A couple of toga-clad ancient Greeks transported through time to present-day England wouldn't look around and ask each other, 'Why are *we* so oddly dressed compared to these normal-looking people?' Remember I said earlier that when I call something 'ridiculous' or 'stupid', I say at least as much about me as the thing I'm critiquing.

A lot of praying goes on in the Bible, and so it's understandable that a Christian would want to pray for people. I approached this woman and asked if I might pray for her knee. It's not supposed to be super-spiritual or ritualistic and I'd like to clarify that my mind had not been fixed on spiritual matters prior to this moment in the day. Indeed, as I walked over to her across the campsite, I was genuinely trying to work out whether it would be feasible to buy an otter to keep as a pet. With this lady's permission, I placed my hand on her knee and spoke a very basic prayer: 'In the name of Jesus, knee be healed...all pain go, now, in Jesus' name.' Basic to the point of being bland as prayers go. And I neither felt nor experienced anything - perhaps because I was worrying whether Derek the Otter would be all that happy with a second floor flat and no garden.

However, this lady said that she felt a fluid-like energy enter her body through her head. It passed through her body and into the knee, taking all the pain away. Not only could she now bend the knee, but she got up on her own and was walking around unaided for the rest of the day - no agony, no hospital. To this day, she remains 'healed'. To this day, I have no pet otter. Not every story has a happy ending.

We're back in the coffee shop and my younger self is flexing in the mirror, waiting for you to fall on your knees and worship Jesus. However, instead you just say, 'So what?' You tell me that you don't think I'm lying *per se*, but a dusting of miracle stories like cinnamon on a Chai Latte doesn't constitute enough proof for you to change your worldview. Well, fine. Be like that.

Let me share another story, whose ending is more frustrating - and not just because there's no satisfactory conclusion to the otter dilemma.

In Chesterfield town centre there is a gentleman's outfitters which carries a rather splendid line in Victoriana - top hats, waistcoats etc. Rakish cad that I am, I took an early constitutional over there one fine morn to procure myself a pair of beautiful burgundy suede boots. This was the first time I'd bought footwear from a place that didn't also sell dart boards and so I was feeling rather posh (pronounced poh-sh). Bear in mind, this is Chesterfield - if you go outside wearing trousers, you're counted as 'upper class'. 'Here comes Downton Abbey!'

a callow youth once shouted at me as I walked down the street in a suit jacket. 'Oi, mate, where are you off to in that - Downton Abbey?!' His follow up punchline was identical to his original joke, but he probably wasn't a professional comedy writer so I let him off. I've also edited out the gratuitous swear words which made up half of his total words.

Purchasing this pair of very expensive, delectable and possibly magic boots excited me so much that I was smiling like the 'after' guy on an *Imodium* advert. In my exuberance, I asked the shopkeeper whether I could return the favour by praying for him.

'Well, I've got real problems with my back, so you could pray for that.'

Once again I wheeled out Healing Prayer 101: 'In the name of Jesus, back be healed. Full restoration and movement restored in Jesus' name. Amen.'

This time I felt heat in my left arm and asked if he could feel the same. 'Yes, I can feel heat and a tingling. I've never experienced anything like this before.'

In my limited experience, this is a very common human response to God 'showing up' in this way. Indeed, there's a story in the *Gospel of Mark* where Jesus heals a paralysed man and the crowd who have witnessed it declare, 'We have never seen anything like this before!'

Where this man had previously been unable to bend, he now could. Later that evening, when I was parading around in my suede boots and *Toy Story* pyjamas while *You're the Best Around* by Joe Esposito belted out from *Alexa*, I got a call from a friend who worked in the same complex as this bloke, to say that 'Brian's been telling all the other shopkeepers that Jesus healed him!'

Why is this a frustrating story? Because Brian wasn't interested in taking it further. I re-visited him several months later and he reiterated that he'd never experienced anything like it. He introduced me to his wife, who said, 'Oh yes, he came home and told me all about the miracle.' But neither of them were looking to explore the deeper meaning of the physical healing. Like a lot of people, they were ambivalent about whatever Big Story was being told and acknowledged they were content to simply have a slightly improved Little Story. They were happy for what was hidden in plain sight to remain that way. For me, that felt like a defeat. I want people to feast at the banquet, not simply to smile approvingly at the set menu. A suede boot can be beautiful to look at, to grip in your hands, to sniff - but it was made to have a foot inside it and for that foot to take it on adventures.

So although I love to talk about healing and miracles, I don't use them as proofs of Christianity.

In my opinion (an opinion I respect and I think we all should) the point of healing is to *point*; to act as a symbol and a signpost through a doorway to another type of world, to a higher form of union and relationship. In Christian thought, God's plan for us all is to have fullness of life through a relationship with him that stretches into eternity, so He's very much in the business of pointing people towards that relationship via a range of different methods, one of which is physical healing. The reason not every prayer for healing is answered with a 'Yes' is because God's aim for us isn't to have a life of unblemished health and limitless wealth so that we never need to call on Him. That's the genie from *Aladdin*. That's not God.

A gentle critic might say here, 'You claim God's not a genie, Andy, but what you've just described from those stories is pure Disney or straight from a J.K Rowling book.' I acknowledge the challenge, but I would want once again to shift the framing slightly; to observe it from a different perspective. I was once watching one of the Harry Potter films with a friend, who paused the film part way through and said, 'If all this was true then maybe I wouldn't be so sad all the time'. What my friend was experiencing, I think, was that word *sehnsucht* - that longing and desire for something seemingly out of reach.

JRR Tolkein said that stories like this are 'the realisation of imagined wonder'. We love *Harry Potter, Lord of the Rings, His Dark Materials* etc. not because they are completely fictional, and certainly not because there really is a Hogwarts or Hobbits, but because they point to a truth that we can't quite grasp, a reality that we desire. But what if that desire itself was 'from the stars', a signpost to something bigger - to another life? Thirst can be quenched because there really are drinks. Maybe the longing that we all occasionally feel for a world beyond ours is not just a weird quirk of evolution.

Quantum Physicist Bernard d'Espagnat called matter a 'veiled reality'. Writer Iris Murdoch says that art (including creative storytelling) 'pierces the veil and gives sense to the notion of a reality which lies beyond appearance.' The idea is this: stories and storytelling, joy and hope and true love's kiss, point to something beyond the physical world. They are, to reference a book in the Bible called *Hebrews*, 'the evidence of things not seen.'

BIBLE BASHING

We're back in the cafe with my younger, less bald self.[7] When the miracle sales pitch didn't work, the fresh-faced Andy might have tried to style it out by saying, 'Ok....well....erm...Ok, well let me talk to you about the Bible.' You wonder if you have time to step in front of the Number 11 bus trundling along the road outside, but you had to finish off my Millionaire's shortbread and now you feel sick. And that was the plan all along, friendo.

I tell you that I think we can show the Bible to be reliable; that it hasn't been doctored or corrupted and that we have, at least, faithful translations of what was written down 2000+ years ago. Obviously, the Bible can be misquoted and taken out of context. For instance, when the Apostle Paul tells his friend

---

7   *My favourite childhood memory is hair. I was once likened to 'a young Jeremy Irons', which is infinitely more preferable than a heckle I got on this latest tour, claiming I resemble 'Lord Voldemort after a nose job.'*

Timothy in one of the New Testament books, 'God has not given us a spirit of fear,' I suspect he wasn't imagining me repeating it on loop whenever I'm walking through a park and a goose looks at me.

In my experience of having animated chats and downright chinwags about the Bible, there are three commonly raised objections:

1   Jesus never existed.
2   People don't come back from the dead.
3   The Bible was doctored long after the events.

What is there to say in response which might be helpful?

In response to the claim that Jesus never existed, I might reference Bart Ehrman, a non-Christian who is without doubt one of the world's leading New Testament scholars. He says that the question of Jesus having lived is 'not even an issue for scholars of antiquity...(because) he is abundantly attested in early sources,' and that claiming Jesus wasn't real 'makes you look foolish' - more foolish than a grown man seeing a small group of geese blocking his path and panicking like it's the evacuation scene from *Titanic*. Bart Ehrman doesn't believe that Jesus was God, but no serious New Testament scholar would doubt his existence.

Next, in response to the idea that people don't come back from the dead, I would largely agree! Nobody is defending or desiring a full-scale zombie apocalypse. The claim isn't that people randomly come back from the dead like a supernatural Whack-a-Mole. The Christian claim is that Jesus was raised from death as a vindication of his personal claim to be God. And I might tell you that the majority of New Testament scholars (a group which is not, perhaps surprisingly, comprised primarily of Christians) believes four established facts about Jesus' resurrection:

1   Jesus was crucified and buried in the tomb of Joseph of Arimathea.
2   His tomb was found empty.
3   After his death, Jesus appeared to hundreds of people, both individually and corporately; what might be termed *post-mortem appearances*.
4   Jesus' disciples really did come to believe that Jesus was raised from the dead and started preaching his resurrection, almost invariably at the cost of their own lives (according to tradition, all but one of the original twelve disciples were brutally executed for their faith in Jesus).

Finally, in reply to the claim that the Bible was doctored long after the events, I might tell you that even the most anti-Christian sceptical scholar will allow that 7 of Paul's 13 letters in the New Testament are authentic (Romans, 1st and 2nd Corinthians, Galatians, Philemon, Philippians and 1st Thessalonians). Authentic doesn't here mean infallibly true; it simply signifies that scholars believe those letters to have been genuinely written by Paul and free from tinkering.

And I may be fairly successful at showing you the reliability of the Bible, because I've read some books and haven't just scrolled a Wikipedia page on Bible hoaxes or watched the Zeitgeist movie. But you could then respond by saying, 'Ok, you've answered some questions, but the most you have done is convince me that a couple of thousand years ago a small group of people genuinely believed that Jesus came back from the dead and were, it has to be said, uncommonly successful at telling people about that, even when their own lives were at stake. But it doesn't mean that Jesus was/is God.' And you would be perfectly reasonable to take that stance. I do love our chats.

The flaw inherent in both my above approaches (miracles and Bible reliability) is that they insert an unhelpful middle man into the proceedings. I'm trying to use something you don't know about or haven't experienced to prove to you that something else you don't know about or haven't experienced is *the* Big Story you've been looking for. I'm using the wrong symbols. My half of the clay *symbolon* doesn't match yours.

So how about this: instead of me relaying wacky stories or randomly quoting scripture at you, why don't we just keep it more simple? Why don't we just take a look at your Little Story. Let's assemble the things you already know to be true in your life and simply ask, 'Is there a Big Story out there that makes sense of your Little Story?' And if so, which one? It's only quite a humble claim. It's tricky to make any worldview completely cohere in the way we would like, so which one makes the most sense? Which comes the closest?

You've worked out by now that your Little Story is the same as mine.

You believe in Unconditional Love: you want to experience someone's unwavering commitment to you, and you don't want to be rejected because of who you are or what you've done.

You believe in Freedom: you don't want to be oppressed or enslaved.

You believe in Purpose: you want your life to go somewhere and to be about something.

You believe in Justice: you do believe that some things really are objectively wrong and other things are objectively, indisputably good. You have what we might call the *human rights urge*.

You know what it means to experience Beauty, Joy and Hope. You know how they *feel*, not just what the words mean.

You believe that Death feels unnatural.

You may be cynical and doubtful about lots of aspects of life, the universe and everything, but you're not a radical sceptic about these things. You see the same doors in the walls of the world that I do.

A phrase often batted around these days is 'The meaning of life is to give life meaning', which sounds great but takes about 10 seconds to expose as the mythical nonsense that it is. Because if the meaning of life is to give life meaning - if life has no fundamental meaning and we just get to invent it for ourselves as we go along - then, to use the obvious example, when Hitler exterminated six million Jews he wasn't doing anything wrong. Hitler was actually just giving his life meaning. Think about it: a little man from Austria captivated the hearts of an entire nation; he took on the greatest powers in the world and nearly won. He was living his best life. And you know who I mean by Hitler, don't you? You don't think I mean Craig Hitler who works at the local golf club and really needs to change his surname, Craig. Craig, seriously mate, it's upsetting the members.

If there is no God and the meaning of life is simply to create our own meaning, then everything is up for grabs. Life is just a big metaphysical all-you-can-eat buffet. Warmongering, cruelty to cats, ritualistic slaughter of traffic wardens - if you can pile it onto your plate and claim it's meaningful to you, who am I to say those things don't constitute a healthy diet? And so Adolf Hitler didn't do anything wrong.

But here's the thing: you think that's obscene. You think the idea that trying to eliminate an entire race of people for personal reasons is *wrong* - bindingly, incontrovertibly wrong. You don't think that exterminating life creates meaning; you know that it tramples meaning because you know that human life is precious. Which should show you that you don't really believe that the meaning of life is simply to give life meaning. Your first words to a rampaging warlord wreaking havoc throughout your hometown wouldn't be, 'You do *you*, hun, xoxox.'

You and I agree that life has meaning, but we don't invent it - we discover it. It's already there and we stumble into it and trip over it and dig for it. It's archeology, not architecture.

Which Big Story makes the most sense of your Little Story? For those of us interested in science, the scientific method is simply about finding a model which best fits the available data. Science isn't about flawless irrefutable proof in the same way that pure mathematics is; science is about *inference to the best explanation*. So, using the data that you have stored in your triple hard-drives of heart, mind and soul, which model from amongst the Big Stories out there best fits that? What's the line of best fit through Love, Purpose, Freedom and Justice? How do we upholster our moral fabric onto the ultimate furniture of the universe? What are our options?

THE NOMINATIONS ARE...

Is it Atheism?

Atheism might be true - any of these stories might be true, of course - but I would suggest that Atheism makes the least sense of your Little Story. If Atheism is true then there is no *ultimate* right or wrong, no justice, no judgement. There's just survival: survive as well as you can, for as long as you can, however you can. So Hitler, one of history's greatest war criminals, actually bested you because he lived out the atheistic truth - that we are merely protoplasmic sacks of chemicals with a limited use-by-date. Anything goes, all things are permissible. As Friedrich Nietzsche said, 'If you gaze into the abyss, the abyss also gazes into you.'

Furthermore, if Atheism is true then, while you do have a purpose, your purpose is to pass on your genes to the next generation - and that's about it. To quote Kool and the Gang, 'Celebrate good times, come on!'

You're also *free* - what philosopher Jean Paul Sartres would describe as 'condemned to be free'. You're free to be a randomly (albeit beautifully) ordered collection of molecules, dancing off against other randomly ordered collections of molecules until you reach your great reward...which is extinction. This is the Good News of Atheism. Whether you die at 92 years of age after a joy-filled life of humanitarian aid work, or you die screaming in pain after 9 minutes, your reward is the same: extinction, annihilation, obliteration. Why? That's easy - because the universe doesn't love you. The universe isn't sure why it invented itself, let alone why you're here.

In a godless universe, we are all gatecrashers at a party who weren't invited and couldn't even be bothered to bring a *Tiramisu*. The cosmos isn't sure why you're here, doesn't care that you are here, and won't be fussed when you leave early to catch your bus back to oblivion. The universe is just not that into you. And remember when earlier I said that Death feels unnatural? Well, on this reading it shouldn't, because Death isn't just a natural part of life - it's actually the great hero of the story!

We believe that Love should win. #LoveWins is everywhere, and we believe it should and we believe it ultimately will. But I'm so sorry, if there is no God then #DeathWins, every single time. Death is the cowboy riding off into the sunset. Death is the bridegroom waiting for us at the end of the aisle. Death always wins, #Always. Astronomer Carl Sagan tried to poeticise it by saying that 'we are all made of starstuff', while Professor Brian Cox calls us to see that 'we are all children of the stars'. I love the beauty of the imagery, but the grim prosaic reality is that we are nothing more than the lingering odour from one gigantic cosmic belch.

Love is not the greatest power in the universe. Freedom is a lie. Hope is a prank. Joy is an arbitrary accident of evolution. The doors in the walls of the world open out onto a gaping chasm of nothingness. And all that might be true.

But at this point you should want to resist. At this point your internal Rebel Alliance should be scrambling its X-wings. Something in you should be saying, 'No, surely it's better than that.' Once again, we agree.

But before I start popping the Champagne, let's be clear that we're not at Chrisitanity yet. There are, after all, a lot of other religions out there beyond the one where God gets nailed to a tree.

I was down in Bath performing the live version of this book. It had gone really well, save for being heckled that I resemble Lord Voldemort after a nose job. After the show I went to the pub with some of the crowd, where a guy from the audience sidled up to me to share his thoughts. Although we were in

Somerset, this man was a Londoner, and was so unfathomably cockney that I expected him to say 'Parklife' after every sentence.

'Look geezer,' he began, 'I really enjoyed your show, but I didn't like the bit where you talked about Jesus being the only way to God - I think that's a bit exclusive.'

'Yes,' I said, 'I agree that it's exclusive.'

'Well,' he responded, growing in confidence, 'I'm a Buddhist and I believe there are many ways to God.'

'That sounds great,' I replied. I hope on some level that's true - it would make things a lot easier. 'So tell me about this God. Describe him to me.'

At this point, you must imagine a small crowd gathering as the flame from the open fire sputtered and the smell of hops permeated clothing and conversation alike. My interlocutor downed a fresh gulp from his pint of *Philosopher's Muse* and continued.

'Well, God is the things you described, right. He or she matches that Little Story you was going on about. She or he is unconditional love and perfect peace and freedom and justice and the like.'

'Charlie,' I said, for 'twas his name, 'I think you're completely right. I agree that God is all of those things.'

The problem for Charlie and people who think like this, though, is simple: Charlie hadn't just described the god of Buddhism. Charlie had just described Jesus Christ.

This is not some self-exultant Christian bias. It's so important to honour and respect people from other belief systems, but part of that process is to understand what these belief systems actually teach, in their own words and on their own terms. All opinions are available, but they're not all equally informed.

Buddhism is an atheistic religion. There is no God (note the big 'G') in Buddhism. Some Buddhists do believe in a god, but they aren't bound to that by their faith. Buddha was a man who lived, and died, and hasn't yet been resurrected. But he was an agnostic - he wasn't sure whether there was a God or not.

Foundational to the majority of the Far-Eastern religious thought which has flooded the West since the 1960s (and from which a lot of the New Age thinking and practise has developed) is the fact there isn't a *personal* God to love you. God is not a person but rather, at most, a *force*. Only a person can love. Impersonal forces can impact you, but they can't love you. So it may seem tolerant and even-handed to say things like 'all religions contain a God of love', but it simply doesn't respect the actual teachings of a worldview like Buddhism which doesn't require a personal God.

We can go even further though. In Buddhism, all physical matter is *maya*: illusory. So nothing matters. For the Buddha, all desire of any kind was bad because it is desire which leads to suffering. So the wish to see justice for abused children would have the same merit as the wish to sleep with another man's wife - they are both desires from which one needs to detach.

Such thinking surely makes a mockery of terms like *good* and *evil*. It also undermines your perfectly *good* desires - to be loved, to live a good life, to find happiness - showing them to be signposts pointing in the wrong direction, doors with no handles. If Buddhism is true, our Little Story is pranking us. *I think, therefore I am,* says Descartes. *I feel, therefore I am deluded,* Buddha might respond.

The reason I can write a book like this in the first place and hold out hope that you have at least read this far, is because I'm acknowledging that you are a real person. I'm catering to your self-evident belief that you exist as a unique entity. I've assumed that you probably believe on some level that life is about being the best *you* you can be, and that you're interested to some degree in the question of what it means to be human. I've gone big on the fact that not only do you have a personal identity, but your personal identity is important. But that isn't an argument that you would find being made in most religious thought. In general, Far-Eastern spiritual thought (comprising the religions of Hinduism, Buddhism and others) can be labelled as *monism* - the idea that everything is *one*. Within that oneness, any sense of human uniqueness is completely refuted. With monism, your purpose is to realise that *atman* (the human soul) and *brahman* (the god force) are one and the same. 'Atman is Brahman and Brahman is Atman'.[8] You are the god force and the god force is you. That sounds amazing, until you realise that God is impersonal, *not* personal. Your end goal, then, is not to become fully human, but actually to dehumanise. Not to find your identity, but to hand it in as an immature daydream. Self-realisation isn't about living your best life, but about understanding that your life has no value in and of itself. That doesn't sound like a Big Story that matches our Little Story. It doesn't sound like Good News.

The great Russian writer Leo Tolstoy wrote that 'where love is, God is'. The reality is that there's only one Big Story out there where God loves you unconditionally. In their own words and on their own terms, other religions don't scratch that itch. In the *Qu'ran*, it says, 'Allah loves not the unbelievers.' If Islam is true, which it might be, then we have a problem. Even if *all roads lead to God*, as my new friend Charlie wanted to claim, and that God turns out to be Allah, then most of us are in super hot water.

What I'm certainly not claiming is that Christians are morally better than people of other faiths - because they most definitely are not. We've all got a dark side - I once threatened to kill a cat for attacking my newly erected Christmas tree. What I am

---

8   *And just to reiterate, I am not Batman.*

saying is that even if Christianity is false it's the only story of Hope for humanity. It's the *symbolon* you've been searching for. That part of your Little Story where you desire to be loved unconditionally is not found in any of these other Big Stories.

Back in the pub, and Charlie was fending off my words with an empty bag of *Quavers* and making goose noises to try and intimidate me. He reiterated that I was being exclusive and I reiterated that yes, in a sense, I was. I think that by not believing every religion to be exactly the same thing, Charlie thought I was being intolerant. But religions are not superficially different yet fundamentally similar. They are, at best, superficially similar and fundamentally different, diverse and divergent. No religion teaches that any of the other religions are fully true. None. They all might be false, but they can't all be true - and they don't claim to be. And we can happily say that all religions - all philosophies, even - contain at least some truth. But, with one notable exception, those truths don't go far enough. They tell the first half of a really good story.

Charlie bristled slightly.

'Come on, man, have some compassion!' he said, errant Quaver shrapnel spraying everywhere.

'That's interesting that you use the word compassion,' I replied. 'So you think that compassion is a real thing - it's a symbol of something?'

'Absolutely. You know what compassion means and you should show some. Parklife!'

The intriguing thing is that the word compassion does have a very defined original meaning. It comes from two Latin words, *com* meaning 'with' and *pattio* meaning 'to suffer'. *To suffer with.* As we've seen though, within Charlie's own worldview the desire for compassion is misplaced, because it is *desire* itself which causes suffering. So why would Charlie exhibit this desire for compassion? Because, I think, the Big Story that Charlie was holding to didn't really match his Little Story - those things he innately knew to be true and desirable. And as someone once said, it's the truth that sets us free.

None of the other epic religious leaders throughout history has preached about Freedom in the way you want Freedom to exist. They weren't able to, because they didn't have security in their identity, and the cause of this identity crisis was that they didn't have permission to know God personally - they weren't granted that access. Again, back in the *Qu'ran*, when talking about the afterlife, Mohammed says, 'I do not know what will happen to me.' Mohammed, the founder of Islam, wasn't sure whether he'd lived a good enough life to get to heaven. And even if he had, the Islamic view of heaven is rivers of wine and sexually available women, which is fantastic if you're a pirate from the 1700s. Oh sure, it's absolutely spot on for seafaring buccaneers! But what if you're a single mother from Luton, or someone struggling with alcohol dependency? I don't think that's good enough. It might be true, but it's not a story of Hope. It contradicts your in-built idea of Justice.

Gandhi, arguably one of the greatest and most noble men of all time, apparently said, 'It is an unbroken torture to me that I do not know my creator.' An unbroken torture. There's a phrase in Hinduism (Gandhi's religion), when asked what God is like, which says 'Na iti na iti.' Not this, not this. It's useful to know that God isn't a ham sandwich or a fire-breathing dragon, but at some point we need to know who exactly God *is*. Because until we know the nature of the Creator, how can we as created beings have any real chance of finding or securing our identity?

Gandhi was expecting to live through hundreds of extra reincarnations, the only common denominator for which would be his own personal suffering, until he reached his great reward which, in Hinduism, is 'the snuffing out of the flame of desire': that point at which we empty ourselves of *all* our desires and get stirred into a soup of senseless impersonality. It might be a blissful extinction, but it's not fullness - it's emptiness. It's death rebadged. And nobody likes soup.

But then a door opens. A familiar looking stranger enters and suggests to you, in hushed tones, that it might be loads better than that. 'You will know the truth, and the truth will set you free.'

'What's the truth, stranger?' we might say. To which he shakes his head with a smile and says, 'Not *what* - *who*. Me. If you've seen me then you have seen the Father (*John* 14: 9). Come to me and, because I live, you will live also (*John* 14: 19).

In Gandhi's unbroken torture comment, in Charlie's request for compassion, we find an unfulfilled longing in their Little Stories. But all we need to do is find the right Big Story. In Jesus, we find it; we see that longing fulfilled. It was a torture for Gandhi not to know God because he *was* created to know him. In the book of *Acts* (Chapter 17) the Apostle Paul, while debating in the great intellectual arena of Athens, points out a tomb 'to an unknown God.' He goes on to say that God is not actually unknown, but made known and knowable in Jesus; that he is 'not far from each one of us'.

Raimon Pannikar, the Indo-Spanish Roman Catholic priest, said: 'We may speak not only of the unknown God of the Greeks, but of the hidden Christ of Hinduism.' That's to say, there is a longing in Hinduism for something that Hinduism itself cannot satisfy. But we know a guy who can.

In practically every people group ever discovered, there has existed a belief in a High God. Someone is on the other side of that door. The Christian claim is that Jesus is indeed this High God, who stoops low, knocks, enters on request, tells us his name and, by revealing his identity, gives us ours.

Philosopher Emmanuel Kant claimed that we could never reach out and grab at ultimate reality. But what if ultimate reality came in and grabbed us? Ludwig Wittgenstein, another mighty philosopher, claimed that absolute truth was beyond the limits of human understanding and morality was just a series of word games. But what if *words became flesh*, turned up in the neighbourhood and said 'It's who you know, not what you know'. What if?

How many Gods offer to suffer with and for you? One.

How many Gods tell you that they love you unconditionally, no matter what you have done? One.

How many Gods tell you that you actually can experience true forgiveness, so that the stuff you've done wrong and the stuff that's been done wrong to you doesn't get to win and have the final say? One.

That you actually can be free and know God personally? One.

That you *should* think death feels unnatural because it wasn't meant to be that way and it won't be like that in the end? One.

It's all the same God. And his name is Jesus Christ.

Charlie was right. Christianity *is* exclusive. It's exclusive because it excludes all the other Big Stories where there isn't a God willing to suffer with and for you, where your cries of pain are either unheard or unheeded. Christianity is exclusive because it rejects every Big Story in which the Creator of the universe doesn't say you're worth dying for.

Frankly, I'll take that kind of exclusivity. And maybe you should, too.

You should happily rule out any Big Story where God isn't that into you, and you should pick the one where He knows you by name and calls you home, offering you an abundance of life. Jesus himself says: 'The thief comes only to kill and destroy; I have come that they may have life, and have it to the full.' (*John* 10:10)

THE CLUES ARE THERE

Every story has a final chapter.

My favourite verse in the entire Bible is *Colossians* 2:15, which says rather awesomely:

'Having disarmed the powers and principalities, He made a public spectacle of them, triumphing over them by the cross.'

What do we mean by powers and authorities? We mean anything dark, any evil in your life that's trying to steal your joy and rob you of your God-given identity. It might be addiction, it might be depression, self-harm, fits of rage. These things are real and you shouldn't be ashamed if you are struggling with them. But at the cross, Jesus takes on these powers. He disarms them, puts Death to death and raises his arms wide in victory.

Whatever your current worldview, you know that Death is your enemy. It's coming for you and, unless something dramatic happens, it *is* going to beat you. But you also know that Death has minions. Addiction works for death, because if addiction goes unchecked it will kill you. Depression is in the employ of death, because if depression goes untackled then it will detach you, paralyse you and potentially take your life. These things are real. But the headline is this: because of the cross, because of what Jesus has done, *they don't get to win*. They don't get to have the final say. They no longer get to define where you've come from, why you're here and where you're going. *He* does.

Jesus is not a symbol of hope. Hope is a symbol of Jesus. Three nouns used to describe God in the New Testament are *love, light* and *life*. Jesus doesn't just possess these qualities; He *is* them.

All roads do not lead to God and, honestly, you wouldn't want them to. You want a story where your value is infinite; where God's love for you is relentless; where all your struggles will count for something and all your tears will be wiped away. And there's one place to go and collect your treasure: that small hill in first century Palestine where X marks the spot.

The cross is the thing that killed Jesus, but it's a STOP sign for everything that's trying to kill you. The cross is a cosmic restraining order against the powers of death and destruction arrayed against you.

Maybe you're thinking, 'This sounds great, so why haven't I ever experienced this love?'

I want to suggest that if you've ever felt longing for Justice; the Unconditional Love of a parent towards a child; the desire for real Freedom and Purpose; the overwhelming awe at a sunset; the unfathomable Joy in moments of your life...then you have experienced Him. Because that's what it means to be made in His image. He has written his moral laws (of Love, Justice, Goodness) on your heart. And *Hebrews* 10:1 says that, 'The law is just a shadow of the good things to come.' It is by entering into relationship with Him, allowing His love to soak through our lives, that we move out of the shadows into the true light.

But you have to choose it. You have to, in some way, come to the cross. Why? Well, because every deal ever made has taken place somewhere. Business deals are done in a boardroom; marriage covenants take place in a church or registry office; if you want to buy an otter to keep as a pet, apparently there's a website where you meet them alone under an aqueduct with a briefcase full of cash...I don't really want to talk about it - I lost a lot of money.

The deal for your soul, for your life, takes place at the cross of Jesus. If you want that fullness of life we've been talking about, that's the place to come. That's where the treasure is: that small hill where X marks the spot. The author of life is inviting you to bring your Little Story into The Greatest Story Ever Told.

I hope you'll reflect on it, that's really all I'm asking. And I hope as you do that you'll start to consider that, perhaps - just maybe - God hasn't been absent from your life. Maybe he's been there the whole time, hidden in plain sight. 'For whatever is hidden is meant to be disclosed, and whatever is concealed is meant to be brought out into the open.' (*Mark* 4:22)

Either way, next time we meet for coffee, you're buying.

THE END?

'THE ROOM WAS EMPTY. BUT THE DOOR WAS OPEN...JUST A CRACK.'

Stephen King, *The Boogeyman*

AUTHOR'S NOTE...

Thanks for reading. I'm aware that there's quite a lot of content in that final third, and it was suggested that I could have filled the book out to 'a proper length'. But why would I want to do that? Just so I can feel smug at producing a mighty tome? The benefit of a short book is that it's over quicker, for both the writer and the reader, so you get that sense of having achieved and finished something. But also that you can go back and read it again if you missed stuff.

More than that, this is the sort of book I would love to see Christian people pass on to their friends, and I wanted to facilitate that by writing something that was funny and interesting but, also and perhaps mainly, short!

The *Hidden in Plain Sight* show which became this book was written as a response to the conversations I was having with friends and randoms, and how those conversations had shifted in tone and subject over the past decade. During the Noughties, when *The God Delusion* was flying high and New Atheism was in the ascendancy, the debate around religion seemed to be confined to, on the one side, atheists telling us how stupid religious people were and, on the other, religious people retaliating by didactically proclaiming and defending Truth with a capital T. It was all very modernist and adversarial, but both sides seemed intent on defeating the enemy rather than really enticing people with a fulfilling story. There's a line in the Christopher Nolan film *The Prestige* where a character says: 'Making something disappear isn't enough: you have to bring it back.' How do you tear down ideas and simultaneously build up the person whose ideas they are?

And now look here, I do believe in Truth with a capital T. But Truth is much more decentralised in this post-post-modern age. And plenty of religious people are in fact stupid. But the big challenge for Christianity as a worldview, as we reach the end of the first quarter of this century, is not Atheism. It's more a vague pick'n'mix spirituality which caters to a sense of emotional well-being and serves the god of self-care. What I have tried to do within these pages is to gently highlight some of the problems with that type of spirituality while offering a solution which doesn't shame or berate. I agree with Martin Goldsmith (in his book *What About Other Faiths?*) that there is no 'mythical common denominator' to all the world religions, but within the human heart there is plenty of common ground to be building on.

You'll notice that there's no talk of 'sin' or 'hell'. That's not because I don't think those conversations are important, but because they aren't the first conversations we need to be having with people of a postmodern mindset. 'Sin' may well be the ultimate problem for humanity, but it's not the burning question for most individuals. In the same way, insulin is great for Diabetes, but you wouldn't inject it into someone complaining of a sprained ankle and just parade away shouting, 'My work here is done!' In short, then, I've simply tried - imperfect as that attempt may be - to answer questions that I think people are really asking, and to reframe the God debate in a way that is less combative and playgroundy. It grieves me when Ernest Hemingway says 'Every thinking man is an atheist', or when Ambrose Bierce - one of the finest writers of short fiction in human history - describes religion as 'a daughter of Hope and Fear, explaining to Ignorance the nature of the Unknowable'. I wonder whether some of that cynicism is birthed out of an entrenched antagonism and blinkered proselytising that parts of the Christian world have been so guilty of. If you've read HIPS as someone who wouldn't call themselves a Christian, I hope at the very least that you've seen my attempt to really think things through, and to draw a line from the knowable to the unseen, not just from ignorance to the unknowable.

In addition, I've tried not to be too jargony, and where I've quoted philosophers I hope it's because the point was relevant and not just to make myself sound eruditer than I am. The concept of a 'Little Story' really originated with Plato and his *Forms*, the idea being that the reason we understand things like Love and Beauty and Trees is because, somewhere outside the physical realm, the perfect embodiment of these ideals actually exists. And when I talk about how Joy and Hope feel, I'm bringing in what Descartes called 'qualia'. But there just didn't seem to be any need to draw attention to those things within the body of the text. Much better to posture and pose during a postscript, don't you agree?

But whilst every generation releases its own zeitgeists, and while yesterday's activist may well be tomorrow's bigot, not everything remains unballasted throughout the ages. Martin Heidegger coined the term 'Dasein': a philosophy referring to the experience of *being* that is peculiar to humans. And it's this that I've attempted to speak from and into.

Being human is to be part of a vast and overwhelming tapestry. But it often feels as though we are on the wrong side of it and all we have is the odd clue, the stray thread, that there is something beautiful on the other side. In Arthurian legend, there's this idea of the *siege perilous*: a seat at the roundtable for the knight who would one day find the Holy Grail. For me, Jesus makes it possible to take that seat at the table. Some of what I've argued for is held passionately yet

provisionally, but in my own quest for truth and meaning I'm happy at this point to hang up my sword and remove my armour. This battle is done.

If you want to keep up to date with what I'm going to do next, you can check out the website at andykind.co.uk. There's also the @andykindcomedy channel on Youtube.

I release new writing every week (including chapters of upcoming books, comedy articles and short stories) over at Patreon. For the price of a cup of coffee, you can support me as a creative and get exclusive access to all the new work. Head over to patreon.com/andykind and take a look.

If you run a church and you'd like to see a live version of this book - or a general comedy show - then please email me: andy@andykind.co.uk

I think that's about it.

All the best.

Andy

A WORD OF THANKS

Huge thanks to Mark McKnight at *McKnight & Bishop* for publishing this book. We worked together on my 2013 book *The Gig Delusion*, and it's good to be back.

Thanks, too, to the people much cleverer than me who read the drafts, told me what to take out and helped me to find what I hope is the right balance of chiaroscuro. Liam Thatcher, Andy Bannister, Cathy Madavan, Glen Scrivener, Toby Isaacson and Steve Burnhope.

Finally, a special thank you to Rachel and James Tweats, who gave me the space to actually start writing the thing - and so much more besides.

x